Intangibles
A Collaborative Catharsis

Published by: Communications Plus

Intangibles
A Collaborative Catharsis

Emma Rose Casady

Karen Bram Casady

One day I'm going to have a daughter and my husband will say,
"You know she gets her attitude from you, right?"
And it will be one of the greatest days of my life.
Internet Meme, Source Unknown

CONTENTS

to our readers   1

untitled/tangibles   2/3

untitled/intangibles   4/5

untitled/bad strawberry   6/7

untitled/God's pocket   8/9

untitled/couch   10/11

untitled/Jonah   12/13

untitled/God camp   14/15

untitled/always   16/17

untitled/cannibals   18/19

untitled/xanax   20/21

untitled/to do list   22/23

untitled/safety net   24/25

untitled/body of work   26/27

untitled/Stanley Fish   28/29

untitled/a short play   30/31

the artist and the author   35

to our readers

"ekphrasis: a rhetorical device in which one medium of art tries to relate to another medium by defining and describing its essence and form, and in doing so, relate more directly to the audience, through its illuminative liveliness" (wikipedia.org/wiki/ekphrasis).

A friend of ours asked whether the pieces of art in this book were done in response to the prose or vice versa. The answer is a surprising no. The 16 pieces of art and 15 prose pieces came into being independently. Neither the artist nor the writer knew of the other's work as it was created. Our friend was responding to *Intangibles* as if the process of ekphrasis had deliberately occurred. It has not. Yet at first glance, it appears as though it has.

One commonality occurs between both the art and the prose and that is catharsis. The artist used the creation of visual work and the author the written word to work through individual, unique states of emotional stasis. As mother and daughter, (Karen and Emma, respectively) perhaps there was some knowledge between us that hinted at where we stood but certainly not enough whereby each other's work was influenced. Thus, each piece was created independently.

And yet when the results of the two processes came together it was as though we had worked as one. Collaboration occurred at the level of universality whereby emotions and feelings swirl but ultimately have a sameness. Presented separately, each piece has the potential to take a reader/viewer on a journey. But, when the art and the prose juxtapose together, they enhance and unite, and jointly illuminate perhaps a more elevated path.

The result is *Intangibles* where pieces of art exist beside pieces of prose and ekphrasis occurs though perhaps not as a deliberate act but as the coincidental and inherent nature of art.

Please enjoy your ekphratic experience.

Emma Rose Casady, artist and Karen Bram Casady, writer

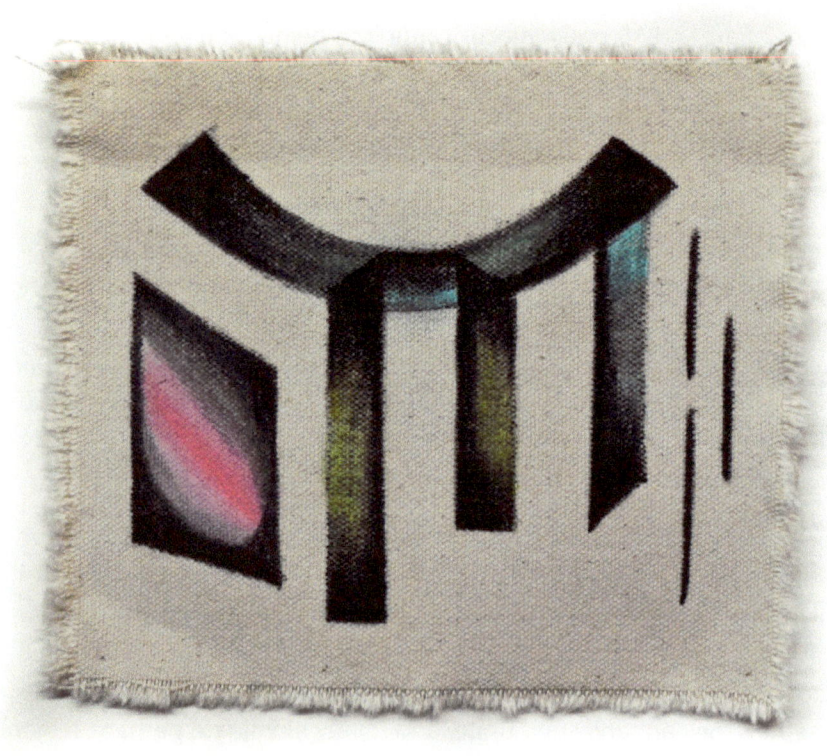

tangibles

the last time God cleared her platter it was tangibles... He lifted his arm and swiped it across her plate... she lost her job... her mother died... her dog died... her daughter moved out...

in the beginning... there was the prequel and then the sequel... and the walking through the in between... that was improv... total improv...

the prequel... she sits next to a campfire... barely burning... only glowing embers... a breath hardly brightens them... she tends it... watches dark clouds gather... waits for the drenching downpour... senses God sitting alongside...

and then the deluge... and her world floats away...

but God picks her up... and drops her... drenching wet... into His pocket... in God's pocket she learns that God has a plan... she thinks about the plan... she stops... she doesn't know the plan... she can't know the plan...

she curls into a little ball... she contemplates nothing... God carries her... she peers out of His pocket... she sees nothing... she never looks up at God... God is unseeable... she eats... she sleeps... she goes through her days...

the sequel... God deposits her on a bit of dry land... she sits in the shade... absorbing the bareness... but for one tiny plant... scrawny but green... when the wind blows it whispers musical notes... and therein she begins again...

she does not recount her days in God's pocket... she does not recount her days rebuilding... she only knows that she added and subtracted... constructed and deconstructed... joined... con-joined... unjoined... rejoined... and in the end a new platter appeared...

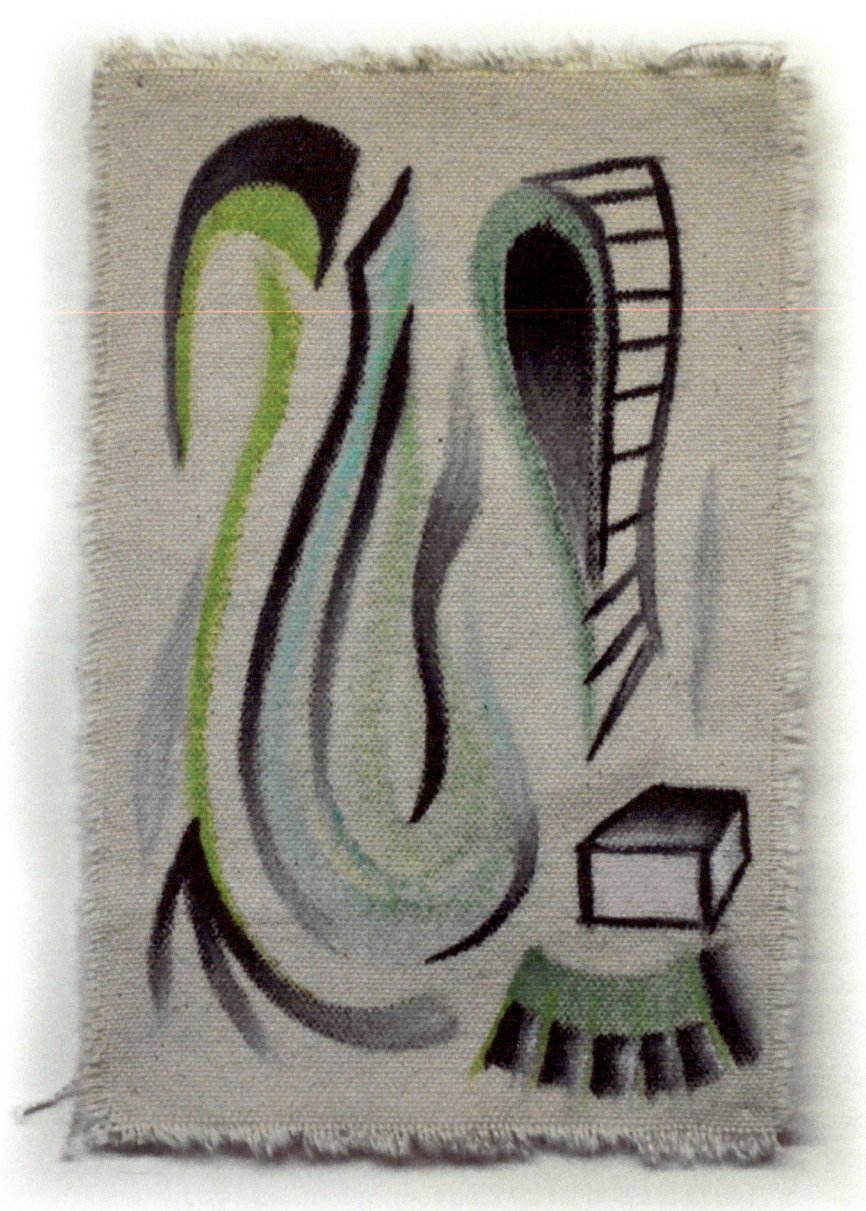

intangibles

this time when God clears her platter it is intangibles... ego and pride... trust and reliability... expectations and possibilities... all stripped away... all smashed... she hovers... she crashes... she lies in anger and resentment on her blown-up bit of land...

she squints into the sunlight... unready to clear the rocks and stones... she looks at the rubble... at the ruin... the improv between the new prequel and the expected sequel... she knows the prequel... everything blows up... the sequel remains unknown... she stares and blinks... maybe sleeps...

she is a metaphor hurled against a wall... crumpled... her life a pile of rubble... a mound of strewn rocks... an IED went off... homemade and hidden... vicious and devastating... she finds this metaphor amongst battle-torn ruins of Mosul... or Aleppo... no bodies except hers... lying in a heap... she thinks she can sit up... she barely opens her eyes...

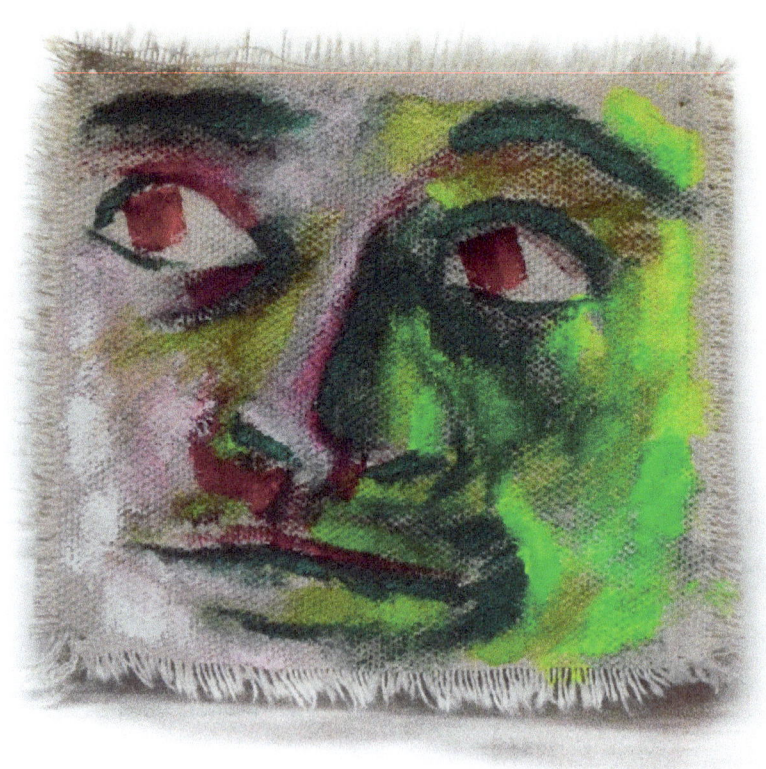

bad strawberry

a tweak a twinge something

odd maybe a bad strawberry maybe

too much caffeine maybe too much

hate maybe too much doubt seizes the

gut cringing with fear looking past transparent

niceness into eyes of malicious evil capable of

devising plots of destruction hiding behind ineptitude

and mindlessness lurking danger get out get out stay no

stay vigilance always vigilance and honesty perpetual

honesty and goodness and compassion mashup

explode out her ass and shatter the glass bowl of her life

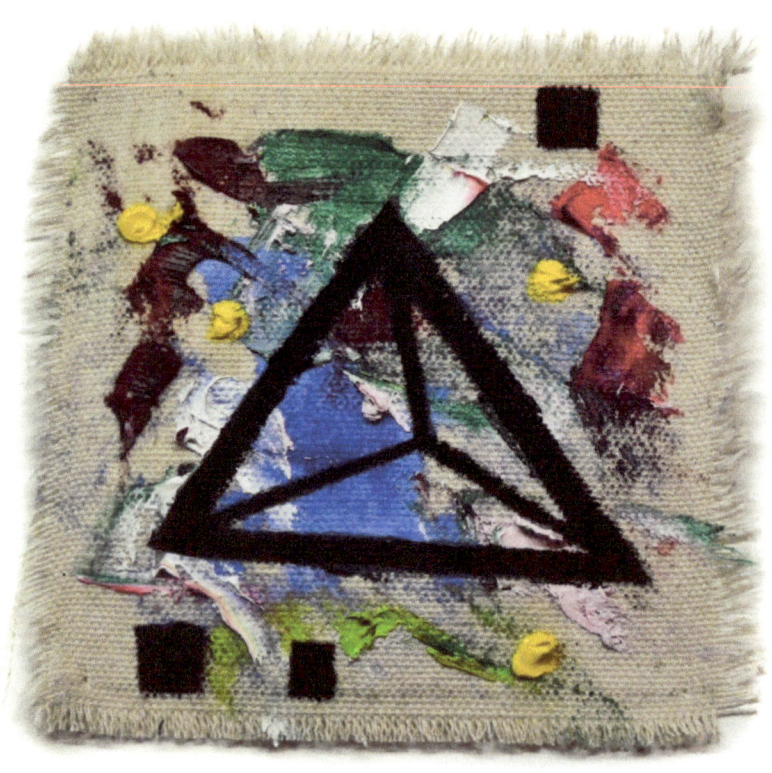

God's pocket

in the old sequel she rides safe in God's pocket... oceans surge around her... God deposits her on an island... she sits under a tree... she contemplates a new garden... in the old prequel she sits next to a barely smoldering campfire... she watches clouds gather... dark and heavy... she waits for the deluge to drown her... funny...

she has shelves and cubbies in her brain... nooks and crannies... laden with her life... she takes stuff down... an idea... an experience... a memory... she looks at it for a while... she puts it back... sometimes she puts a new thing on an old shelf... sometimes it gets a new shelf... sometimes it goes onto a shelf with like-minded things... all things gather dust on her shelves...

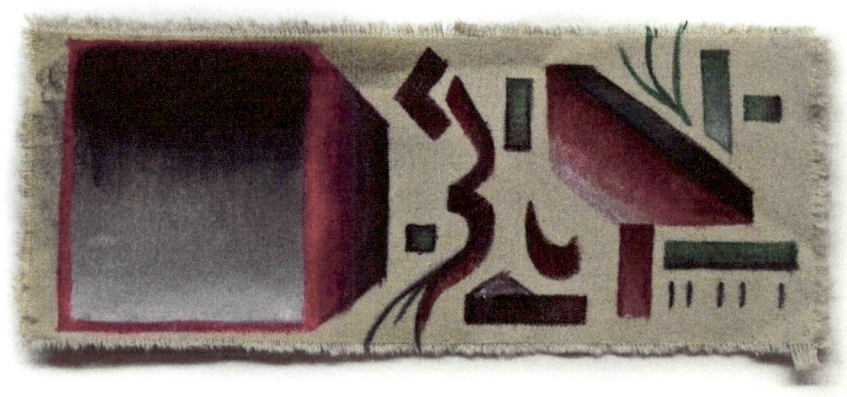

couch

it sags in
  one spot
    at the end
      where she sits
and it tells her stories
of better days and burning incense and
    candles

of Christmas cookie crumbs and hidden nickels
of lost rings and drafts of milky builder's tea and
    sips of wine

it gossips about cousins and ne'er do wells and
    illicit love children

it snickers at its own jokes about muffled farts
and oversized bottoms and the occasional spills and
    cat vomit

it cradles her
  at the end
    in one spot
      as she sleeps

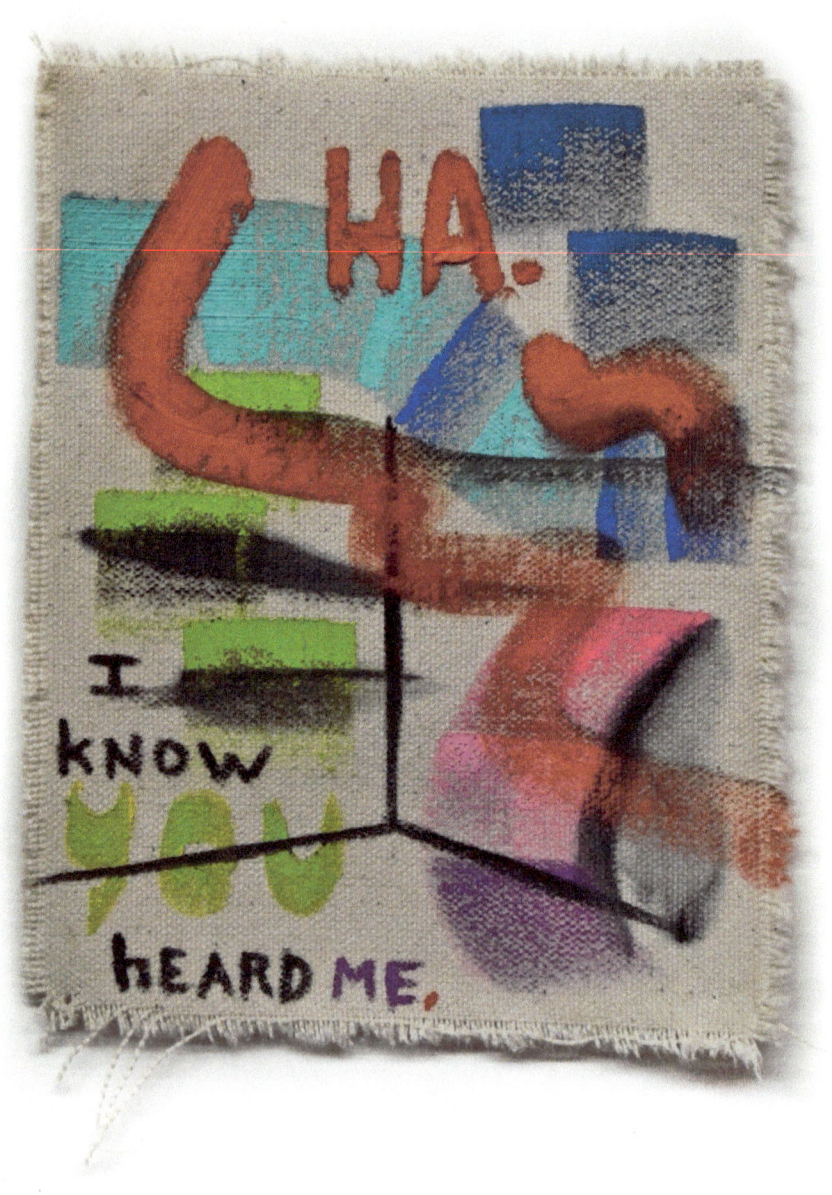

Jonah

she is a metaphor treading water...

splashing and struggling... where is the lifeguard... where is the island... where is God to pick her up by her collar... kicking and screaming... and put her into His pocket once again...

she is a metaphor treading water...

spitting and sputtering... rocky waters roll around her... an undertow grasps at her feet... pulled by peace at any cost and stayed too long... aided by defy her broken barely-wired-together heart and declare love... she prefers the crumpled-against-a-wall metaphor... less tiring... her chances are better... where is God's pocket...

she is a metaphor treading water...

God sends a big fish... she gets gobbled up... she stays for three days in its belly... she meets Jonah... she is Jonah... God loves fools... He forgives them... she is left holding a bag of crushed smelly emotions... she shows God... God throws her back in the sea...

she is a metaphor treading water...

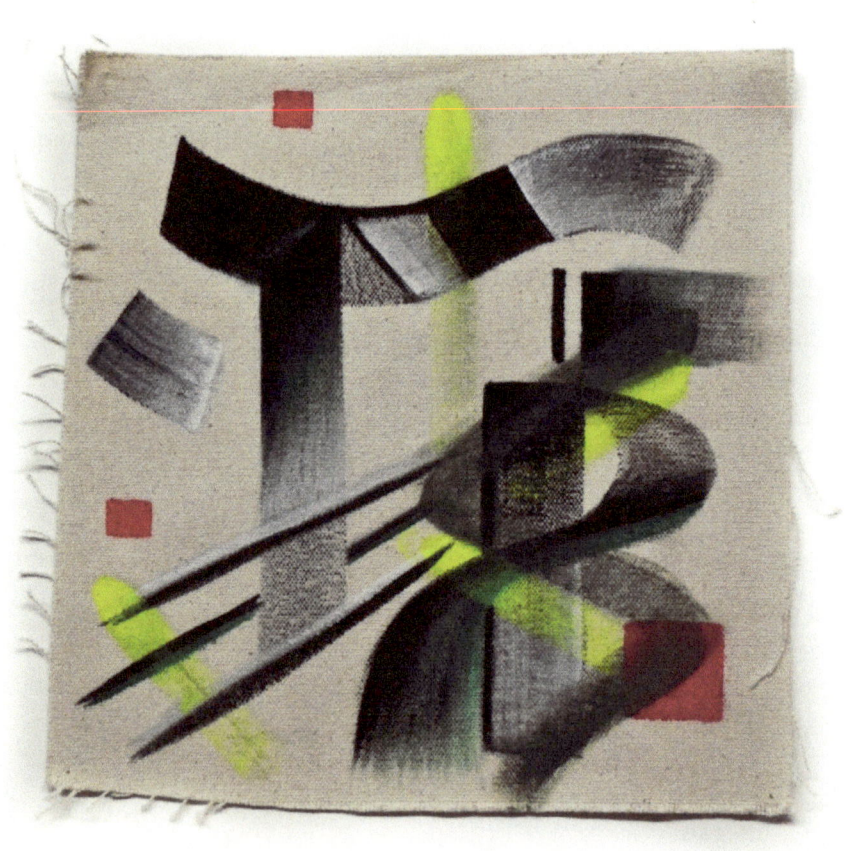

God camp

once she went to God camp... she stayed there when her father died...
she had more energy then... God camp involves interest... God camp
involves activity... God camp heals... rest and serenity between stints of
bustle... details elude her... it works at the time... God camp is a good
place for her now...

peace at any cost and stayed too long... fix one and the other gets
worse... balance one and the other falls out of kilter... stabilize father's
kidneys his heart fails... stabilize father's heart his kidneys fail... he dies...
now she is a computer that has crashed... she is still operating... she is in
safe mode...

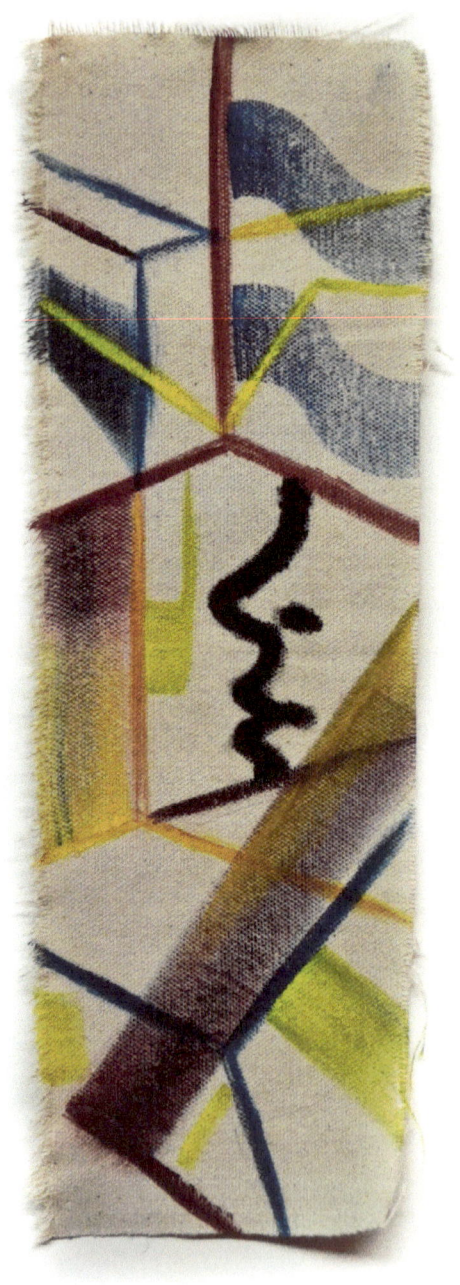

always

always vigilant

always watches

always waits

always seeks

looks around the corner

always strains

always taunt

always in the crosshairs

always ready to run

on your mark get set go

ready aim fire

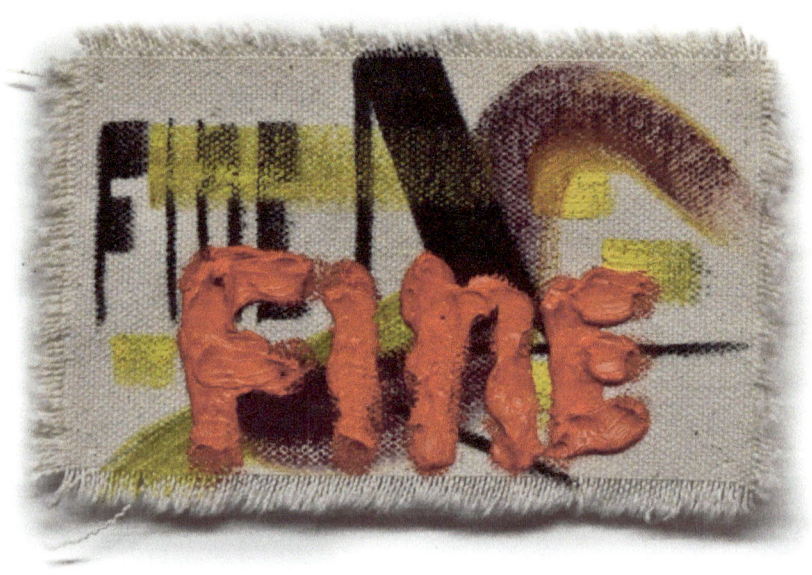

cannibals

her immediate world informs her life... the ups and downs... the ins and outs... day-to-day stuff... none of which has anything to do with cannibals...

anthropophagy – the eating of human flesh; cannibalism...

that subject comes purely from her imagination... write about something completely the opposite of humanism... cannibalism pops into her head... humans eating other humans... anthropophagy... a crazy word for a crazy act...

> FRANK
> Mmmm. Delicious. It's my favorite part. (He lifts his bone up to admire it.)
> DAVE
> Your favorite part? You must be kidding.

> FRANK
> No. No kidding. Elbow is my favorite. You can gnaw around the bone. Scrape off the meat with your teeth. There's something biblical about eating elbow.

> DAVE
> I see your point. I guess I could get into elbow. But seriously, it's just not meaty enough for me and I never feel full after eating elbow. Even if I eat both. Now upper arm. That's another thing. Meaty. Biblically meaty with just the right amount of fat. And the muscle. Well, that's like spaghetti. Yeah like eating spaghetti and meat sauce. If you eat it right.

she takes the snippet and writes a play... her wasted brain attacks the story with vigor... the action soothes her... the most troublesome state of her mind is anxiety... this stems from hardwiring... the ancient concern of abandonment... no one can fix it...

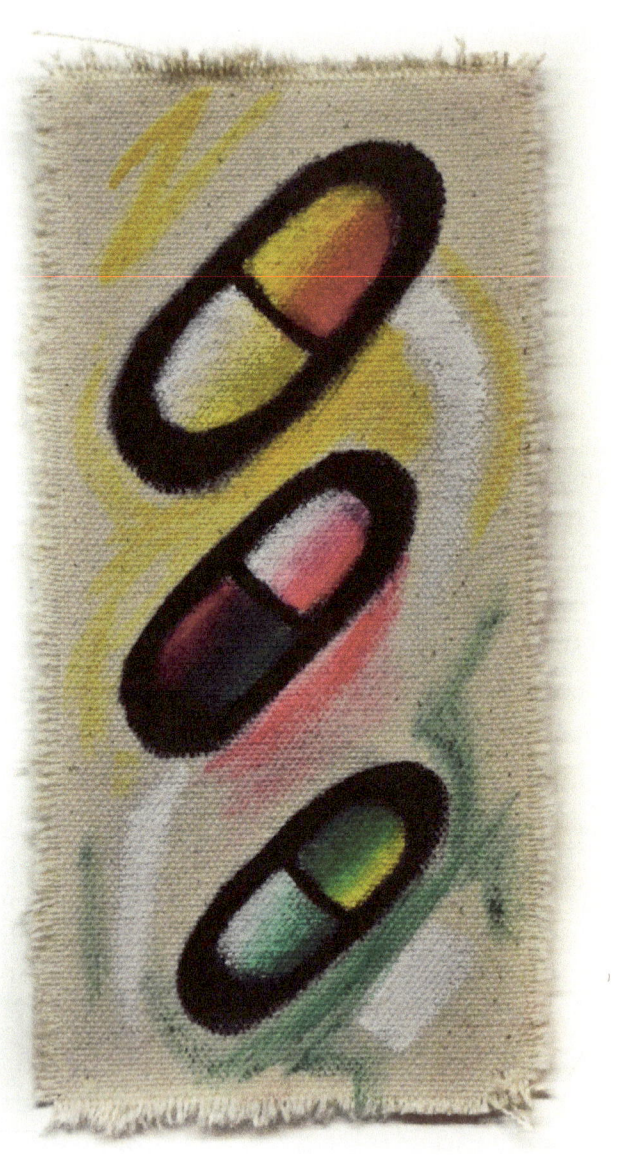

xanax

she reverts to an old mode... pretends nothing is wrong... on the surface nothing is wrong... everything just hums along... she eats dinner... she watches tv... the preacher thunders... do not block out God's light... she can't imagine that she or anyone else can get in the way of God's light... no one has that power... she decides to let God do his job... she goes back to God camp...

a life left in bits and pieces... she picks up the fragments... tries to put it back together... she decides to move on... she has no inkling what that looks like...

she pulls herself together... she goes about her business... but she spins... normal throws her... she pretends that's okay...

she has a huge hair up her ass... she itches for a fight... she needs adrenalin... needs it coursing through her veins... needs to revel in the headache that follows...

she takes xanax... she never takes xanax... xanax relieves her pounding anxiety... xanax titillates her opioid receptors... makes them crave more xanax... they scream xanax in their agony... she resists...

she begins a grateful list... alphabetical... starting with "A"... today she is grateful for air... today she is grateful for her hound... she doesn't make it past "H"...

she drifts... stuff no longer gets handled... she looks at it... wonders about it... thinks about what she might do... could do... but never does... stuff drifts...

she makes a list... puts things in order... crosses things off... hopes for solace... a sense of control... it doesn't work anymore...

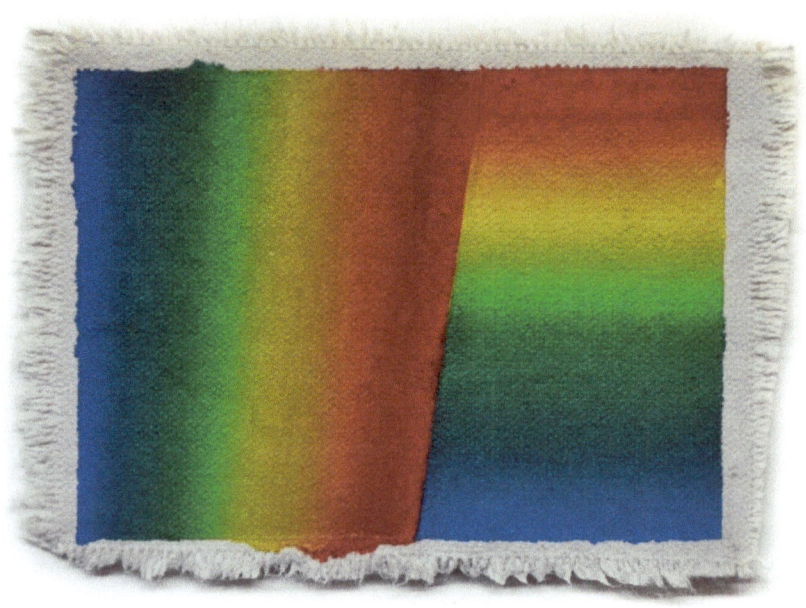

to do list:

        take the car for service

        make a dermatology appointment

        make an eye doctor appointment

        call Afam

        fix it fest

        renew passport

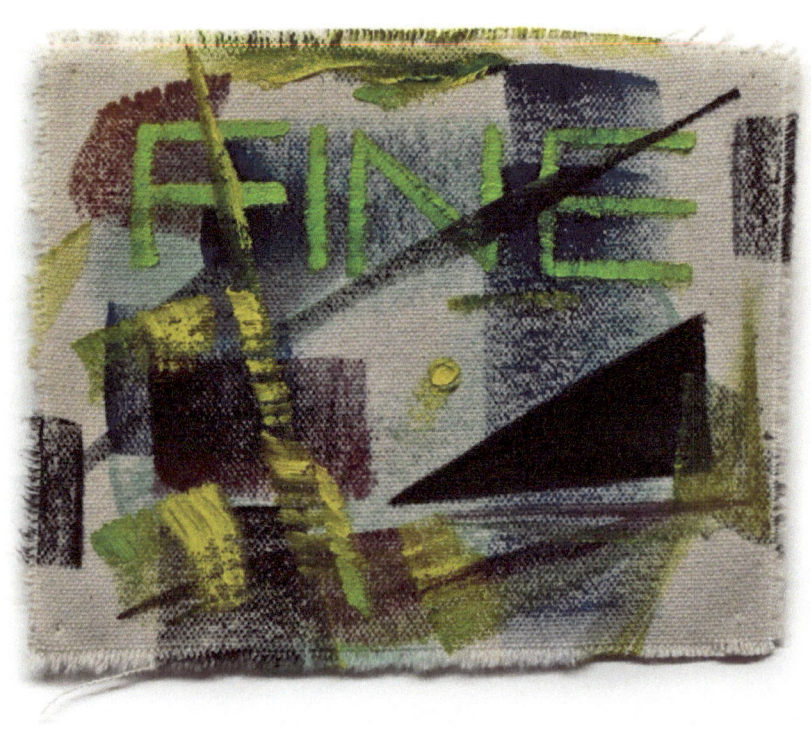

safety net

shell-shocked... blown around... wafted back... sucked forward... she lies crumpled against a wall... like an injured dog... in pain she bites anything and everything... she licks her wounds... she hopes her saliva can heal them...

things that bolster her... now notches on a prayer wheel... spinning around... every so often she reaches for one... hoping it will soothe her...

she prays for her safety net to hold...

she lights incense... she breathes in... she makes a cup of tea... she savors the taste and warmth... she walks... she moves her body... endorphins feed her hungry opioid receptors... stimulate contradictory serotonin...

she picks up a pen... lays her hand upon a page... unfolds her laptop... moves her fingers across the keys... feels the physicality of her brain engaging... of watching it work... she stays in the moment... she is still intact...

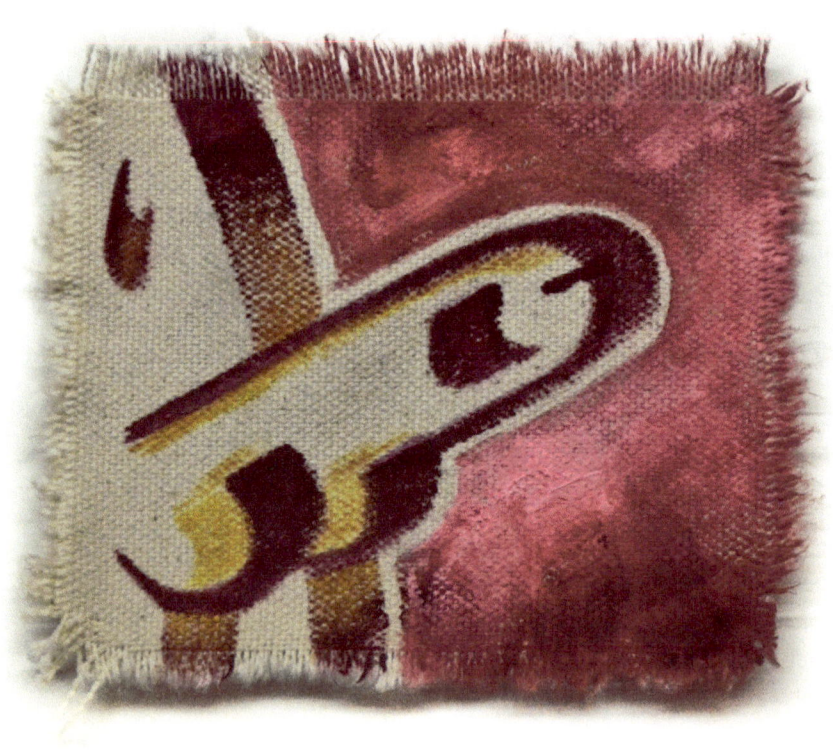

body of work

she looks for a prompt... she thinks, "beds are for sex and sleep"... she is doing neither... she moves to the couch... she sleeps... she wakes... she feels like a turd... chewed up... churned around... shat out... turd becomes a perfect metaphor...

she takes one of her short stories... she converts it to a play... she submits it to a one-act festival... she never hears back... she writes three or four poems... they offer release from niggling torment... she acquires a painter... they take one of her poems... they submit a proposal for a mural... they never hear back... they fuck on her bed... it becomes a writing prompt...

she composes scathing emails... words jump off the page... her fists flail... she pommels the recipients... she revels in the writing of them... accomplishments of hate and disgust... her painter illustrates them... she creates a chapbook of takedowns... she calls it *Ekphrasis*... no one buys it... art elevated...

she flits about... she creates blogs... she fills notebooks... she turns out tomes... she indulges... she dabbles... and every letter of every word... splattered across pages... embedded on screens... adds up... and ripens into a body of work...

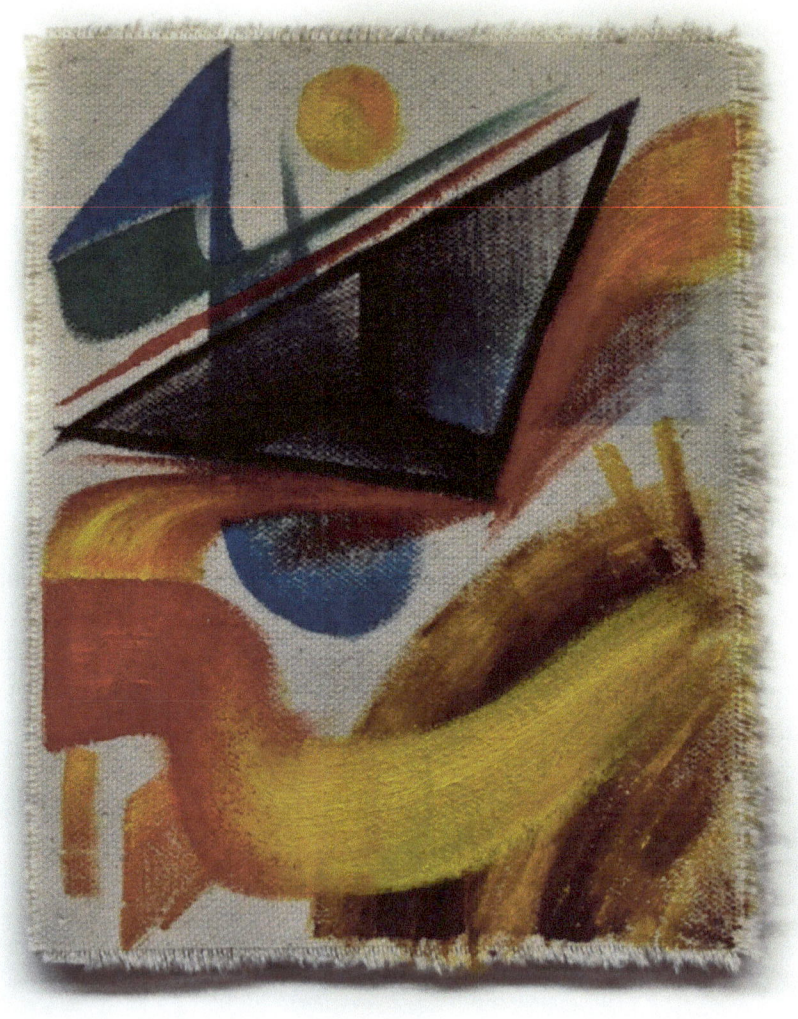

Stanley Fish

she listens to voices describe young writerly lives... one dabbles in fantasy fiction... another writes poetry focused on nature... she bows her head in reverie... the visual artists join in... photographers certain of what they like to photograph... painters certain of what they like to paint...

some asked what is creative writing... and some said nearly everyone has at their disposal the tool of writing... and she said Stanley Fish wrote a shopping list on a chalkboard... and his class interpreted it as clever poetry... and some said what would the Academy think... and she said Stanley Fish is the Academy... and then she writes a play...

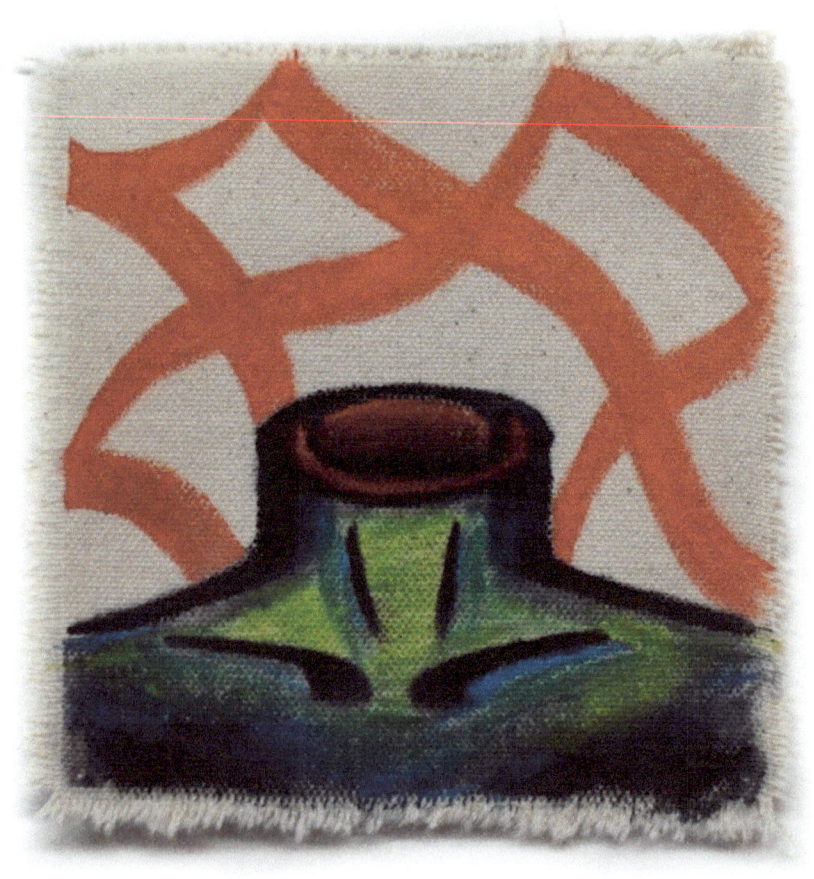

a short play

APOSTATE 1
The academy wouldn't like it.

APOSTATE 2
The academy?

APOSTATE 1
The academy. The establishment. The ivory tower. You know, man.

APOSTATE 2
I can't stand the academy. Stuffy sons of bitches.

APOSTATE 1
They set the standard. They elevate art.

APOSTATE 2
They are full of shit.

APOSTATE 1
They are theoretical. They know better than you or me.

APOSTATE 2
They are dictators. They are predictors. They are assholes.

APOSTATE 1
Don't let them hear you. They have tap dancers hidden everywhere.

APOSTATE 2
Tap dancers? And what about hedgehogs. Ha!

APOSTATE 1
Hedgehogs? Man quit trying to be funny. It's just tap dancers.

   (A hooded priest enters with a bullhorn crooning Frank Sinatra.)

APOSTATE 1
Shit! They're here. They've heard you.

APOSTATE 2
They did not. And he's harmless. I feel his vibes.

APOSTATE 1
No man. That's how it starts. You think you're safe. Priest and all. Next thing you know they've covered you in green sea weed shit and you're suffocated. Dead.

APOSTATE 2
Yeah? Well where are the tap dancers? Why send a crooning priest?

APOSTATE 1
Anathema man. Anything but elitist.

APOSTATE 2
Yeah sure. I don't buy it.

APOSTATE 1
Well buy it man. Look on the horizon. Tap dancers!

APOSTATE 2
Yeah! Wow! Just like the Rockettes!

APOSTATE 1
Yeah! Wow! They'll kick the shit out of you and when they're done pieces of green seaweed shit hail down from the sky.

APOSTATE 2
Personally, I love to eat green sea weed shit.

APOSTATE 1
It covers you. Suffocates you. You can't eat your way out.

> (The crooning gets louder. There is a projection of the Rockettes. Sea weed/confetti floats down onto the stage covering the two actors. They struggle, try to eat their way out, are overwhelmed and die. The Rockettes disappear. The crooning stops, and another hooded priest enters the scene.)

PRIEST 2
(Removes his hood.) They were so promising.

PRIEST 1
Yes. They were. Next time, your turn to croon. I'm almost beginning to like Frank Sinatra.

PRIEST 2
You mustn't say that.

PRIEST 1
I'm thinking to write an essay. A proposal to elevate Sinatra.

PRIEST 2
It won't get past the provocateurs and you'll likely be rehabilitated. Sinatra! What could you possibly be thinking.

PRIEST 1
He's intoxicating.

PRIEST 2
I'll pretend I didn't hear that. Let's get these apostates out of here.

> (They drag off the sea weed/confetti covered bodies. A slight hum of Sinatra is heard. A quick flash of Rockettes appears and disappears.)

THE ARTIST

Emma Rose Casady was born and raised in Los Angeles, California where she lived until the age of 18. After graduating high school in 2012 and receiving high honors in her class for the visual arts, she moved to Albuquerque, New Mexico to pursue a degree in art studio at the University of New Mexico. During her time at UNM she began painting and fell in love with the medium. Emma graduated with her BFA in spring of 2017 and continues to live in Albuquerque where she creates her artwork. For more information about her art, please visit her website at: emmarosecasady.weebly.com

THE AUTHOR

Karen Bram Casady, BA, MA is a poet, short story writer and playwright. Her poetry and short fiction appear in *Manuscript 46*, *Manuscript 47*, and *Manuscript 50*, the online literary journal of Los Angeles Valley College and *The Northridge Review,* the literary magazine of California State University, Northridge. *Intangibles* is her second book of poetry. Her first collection, *Effervescent*, was published in 2015. Other unpublished poetry collections include *Dailies, FridgeDoorPoetry, SlowDrive, SundryAsides* and *Disparate Characters*. She is a graduate of the University of Cincinnati (BA) and the University of Southern California (MA). She is currently working on her MA in English/Creative Writing at California State University, Northridge. She expects to graduate in December 2018.

www.ingramcontent.com/pod-product-compliance
Lightning Source LLC
Chambersburg PA
CBHW040817200526
45159CB00024B/3019